THE PARANORMAL THROUGHO[UT]

DEMONIC POSSESSIONS

IN HISTORY

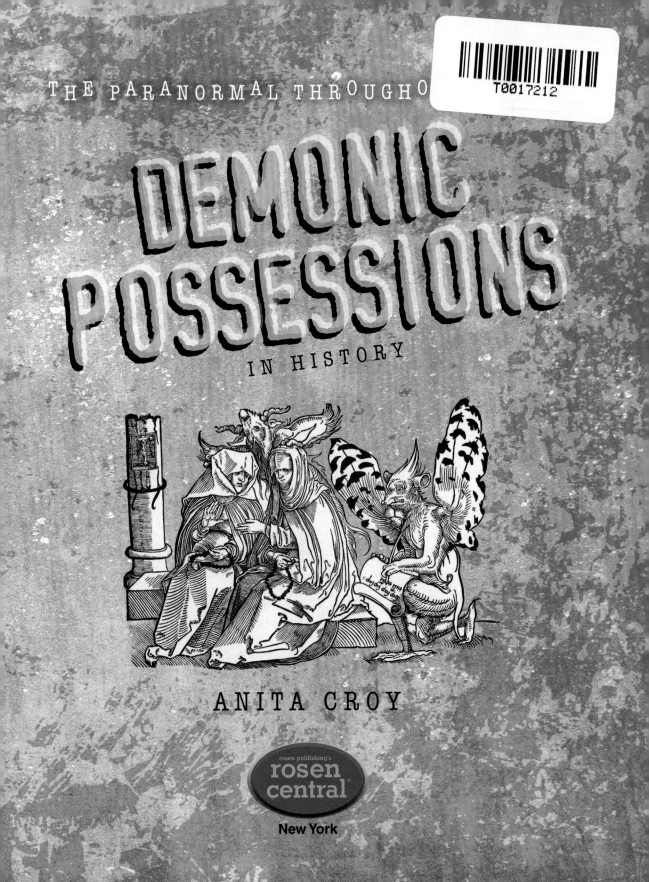

ANITA CROY

rosen publishing's
rosen central

New York

Published in 2020 by The Rosen Publishing Group, Inc.
29 East 21st Street
New York, NY 10010

Produced for Rosen by Calcium Creative Ltd
Editors for Calcium: Sarah Eason and Harriet McGregor
Designer: Paul Myerscough and Lynne Lennon
Picture researcher: Rachel Blount

Photo credits: Cover: Shutterstock: Udra11; Inside: Shutterstock: Benedix:
p. 40; Celiafoto: p. 41; Everett – Art: p. 31; Everett Historical: p. 39; Kit
Leong: p. 37; Min Jun Kim: p. 36; N_defender: p. 38; Richard Peterson:
pp. 42–43; Renata Sedmakova: pp. 8–9; Keith Michael Taylor: pp. 4–5t;
Wellcome Collection: pp. 11, 12, 22, 23, 25bl, 26; Wikimedia Commons: p. 15,
21, 28–29; © Pierre André: p. 6; Hans Baldung: p. 14; William Harvey (1796–
1866): p. 35; Nicholas Hilliard: p. 13; Hector Hyppolite: p. 7; Museo del Prado:
p. 16; National Museum of World Cultures: pp. 32–33; PHGCOM, remade with
F Lamiot: p. 5t; PumpkinSky: p. 27; Sprenger, Jakob: p 10; Sebastiaen Vrancx:
p. 19; Hans Weiditz: pp. 1, 20; Robert W. Weir (photograph courtesy Architect
of the Capitol): pp. 24–25t; Wellcome Collection: p. 30; Zereshk: p. 34.

Cataloging-in-Publication Data

Names: Croy, Anita.
Title: Demonic possessions in history / Anita Croy.
Description: New York : Rosen Central, 3030. | Series: The paranormal
throughout history | Includes glossary and index.
Identifiers: ISBN 9781725346628 (pbk.) | ISBN 9781725346567 (library bound)
Subjects: LCSH: Demoniac possession—Juvenile literature. | Exorcism—
Juvenile literature.
Classification: LCC BF1555.C79 2020 | DDC 133.4'26—dc23

Manufactured in the United States of America

Cover: Some people believe demons can be driven out of possessed people by
Christian symbols such as the cross.

CONTENTS

CHAPTER 1

POSSESSED BY DEMONS

Since ancient times, people have believed that demons, or evil spirits, can take possession of living people. Cave paintings more than 15,000 years old contain depictions of strange figures that some modern experts believe represent either demons or people in the grip of possession. The ancient civilizations that arose from about 5000 BCE all believed in magic and accepted it as part of their everyday lives.

The creatures in this ancient Australian cave painting may represent evil spirits.

Ancient Demons

More than 5,000 years ago, the ancient Mesopotamians who lived in the area of present-day Iraq believed people could be possessed by evil spirits. Other Mesopotamian peoples and their neighbors who lived between the fourth and first millennia BCE, such as the Sumerians, Babylonians, Hittites, and Assyrians, believed people could become possessed in all kinds of ways. They might be placed under a curse or they might be possessed following an action such as stepping over a dead body.

The Evil Eye

The ancient Mesopotamians believed demons caused sickness, and had to be kept at bay. The Mesopotamians also feared witches, or men and women who could perform harmful magic. For protection against demons and witches, people wore charms called amulets and carried out exorcisms, or ceremonies to banish evil spirits. The ancient Egyptians used similar methods to keep good and evil in harmony.

Classical Ideas

The ancient Greeks made a distinction between magic and religion, or the worship of the gods. They believed religion was more powerful than magic, which was a supernatural power to control events. The Romans believed in the existence of witchcraft, which they saw as being always harmful. They were the first people to make many types of magic illegal.

The Mesopotamians believed in birdlike demons that could possess people with a magical stare called the evil eye.

Magic Spells

The Mesopotamians kept demons at bay by writing magic spells on clay tablets using the world's first form of writing, called cuneiform. One such spell banished demons from a particular house. It also forbade them to return for the whole of eternity.

5

ANCIENT DEMONS

The ancient world was full of all kinds of demons. Their presence in many cultures across the globe was rooted in an ancient belief that life was a constant conflict between good and evil.

Demons took different forms depending on where in the world they appeared. In ancient India, the Hindu religion was based on the Vedas. These holy writings described a battle between good and evil. It was a battle between the Asuras, who were demonic spirits, and the benevolent, or kind, Devas. The Asuras controlled the underworld. The Indians wanted to keep the Asuras away, so they made offerings to the many Hindu gods to ensure they were protected. This was the first time demons were said to be the direct opponents of the gods. Later, in Christian belief, the Asuras were replaced by Satan and Devas by God.

According to Indian myth, the Devas and Asuras waged a constant war for control of the world.

I Feel Sick

Early forms of Christianity often made a link between demons and sickness. At the time, people blamed sickness on an imbalance in the body caused by demons. To cure a sick person required getting rid of those demons. In Judaism, demons were said to use sickness to torment humans as part of their battle against God.

World Demons

In the ancient world, demons were believed to take all kinds of forms. Different demons had different ways to torment humans.

The serpent god Dambala (*see below*) is just one of a number of spirits the Haitians call *loa*.

An Ancient Victim

Hypatia of Alexandria was an ancient Greek mathematician, astronomer, and philosopher, and a respected teacher. However, in ancient Greece she was also a woman in a man's world, and many men were jealous of her. Men started a rumor that Hypatia was so gifted because she was possessed by evil spirits. Hypatia paid with her life: she was murdered by a mob in 415 CE.

Often, they appeared as strange animals with tails, pointed ears, or horns. At other times, demons were hard to tell apart from the angels, who were good spirits who lived in heaven. Some of the most evil demons included an African demon who rode a black horse, and Dambala, an evil serpent god from the voodoo religion of Haiti.

CHRISTIANITY

The rise of Christianity led to an increasingly two-sided view that saw the world as a battleground between good and evil. Good was represented by God, Jesus Christ, and the angels, while evil was represented by Satan, the demons, and witches. In Christian teaching, Satan wanted to take control of God's creation. The Bible contains many references to demons.

In this Biblical painting, Jesus is shown driving away a demonic spirit as angels look on.

As Christianity developed, it adopted many elements from earlier religions of the Middle Eastern region. From Persia, it took the idea that the universe was divided between good and evil, with demons and witches serving evil. From Mesopotamia, it took the idea that people should be afraid of demonic possession, and from Judaism it took the belief in a single god who was a force for good. The Romans, who adopted Christianity as their official religion in 380 CE, brought to the religion their view of witches as beings who were purely evil.

Magic Lives On

As Christianity spread, it absorbed ideas from traditional European religions, including the belief that superstition and magic could help people. In 476 BCE, the Roman Empire fell to its enemies, led by the German warlord Odoacer. Europe entered an unsettled period of about 600 years known as the Dark Ages.

During this time, Christianity and superstition were some of the few constant parts of people's lives. People still believed magic potions could cure disease, but the belief in magic now also had a dark side. According to Christian teaching, anyone who could practice magic was capable of causing great harm as well as great good. When crops failed or disease broke out, many people believed it was the work of demons or witches. The Catholic Church became determined to stamp out these old superstitions.

The Bible Speaks

The Church used lessons from the Bible to teach that there was no place in the world for magic. The book of Exodus in the Old Testament contained the order, "You will not allow a witch to live." The Bible also contained a number of different accounts of Jesus Christ driving out demons from individuals.

9

CHAPTER 2
MEDIEVAL POSSESSIONS

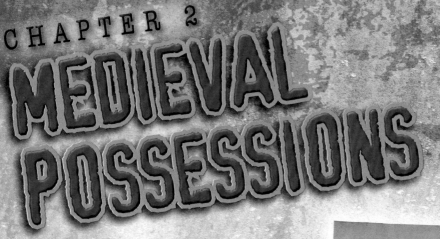

During the Middle Ages, from about 500 to about 1500, the fear of demonic possession was great. People believed that those who worked with the Devil could achieve power over their neighbors. These people were increasingly identified as witches—and some suffered terribly as a result.

A New Fear

After about 1450, the fear of witches became widespread across Europe. Witches could be both men and women, but the people most often accused of witchcraft were older women, particularly those who lived an isolated lifestyle, without being involved in community events. Witches were said to have special powers such as healing or even flying. The Church started to persecute anyone it suspected of being a witch. Most of those who were accused were innocent.

The book *Malleus Maleficarum* was a guide for how to identify and punish witches.

Flaming the Fires

Anti-witch hysteria was whipped up by the publication of *The Hammer of Witches* (*Malleus Maleficarum*) in 1487. The book was the first study of witchcraft, with details about how to spot a witch and how to protect yourself against them. The book helped inspire a series of very brutal witch trials. A second book, *Handbook of Witches* (*Compendium Maleficarum*), was published in 1608. Both books were based on the writers' imaginations along with the confessions of accused witches who had been tortured.

The Devil's Work

People believed witches supported the Devil in return for him teaching them black, or evil, magic. Witches were believed to worship the Devil in ceremonies that mocked Christian rituals worshipping God. The Church accused anyone who did not accept its teachings of working with the Devil.

This painting shows a popular view of how witches lived, mixing magical potions in their homes.

THE TRIALS BEGIN

In 1562, Queen Elizabeth I introduced a law in England to make witchcraft punishable by death. In 1566, Agnes Waterhouse became the first woman in England to be executed under the new law. Of course, she was not the first woman in the world to meet this awful fate.

A Religious Crime

Witchcraft had been considered a heresy, or religious crime, by the Catholic Church since 1484, when Pope Innocent VIII had denounced the practice. The fear of witches took hold across Europe. The words of the Book of Exodus— "You shall not suffer a witch to live"—became the basis for witch trials across the continent. Between 1450 and 1700, around 200,000 witches were killed by being tortured, burned, or hanged. The people who were killed were almost all women.

This woodcut shows two witches with a "familiar," a demon that carries out a witch's orders (*see opposite*).

Finding Witches

In England, Queen Elizabeth introduced the death penalty for witchcraft as a way to stamp her authority on her country and display her support for the Protestant faith. One of her closest advisors, Sir Walter Raleigh, convinced her that witches were controlled by the Devil. Elizabethans used different ways to identify a witch, such as looking for facial marks such as warts or hair on the upper lip. Any woman who kept a cat could be a witch, because cats could be "familiars," which were spirits said to carry out evil activities at the witch's order.

Queen Elizabeth's own mother, Anne Boleyn, had been accused of being a witch.

Mother Waterhouse

In 1566, Agnes Waterhouse, also known as Mother Waterhouse because she was old, was put on trial with two other women, including her daughter. She was accused of using witchcraft to kill a man and of possessing a familiar in the shape of a spotted cat named Satan. The chief witness against Mother Waterhouse was a 12-year-old girl named Agnes Brown. She claimed to have been threatened by a black dog that looked like a demon with horns.

THE TRIER WITCH TRIALS

The largest witch trials of the late Middle Ages took place in Germany between 1581 and 1593. Between 368 and 1,000 people were executed for witchcraft in and around the city of Trier. The killings remain one the biggest mass executions to take place in Europe in peace time.

A Frenzy of Suspicion

When Johann von Schönenberg became head of the Catholic Church in Trier in 1581, he set about ridding his diocese, or territory, of all the enemies of the Catholic Church. These enemies included Protestants, Jews, and witches. Von Schönenberg whipped the local population into a frenzy of suspicion. Between 1587 and 1593, 368 people were burned alive for witchcraft in 22 villages. Many victims were women. By 1588, two villages were each left with just a single woman living in them. Men and children were also put to death, as were both nobles and peasants.

Anybody who objected to the punishments was also put to death. By the time the executions were over, Trier had lost all its leading figures who had tried to speak out against von Schönenberg's leadership, including the rector of the university.

This scene shows an artist's idea of how witches behaved at their gartherings, or sabbats.

Using Torture

In order to secure a guilty verdict, accused witches were tortured with a range of vicious devices to try to make them confess what they had done. The items included thumbscrews, which were tightened to slowly crush a person's fingers and thumbs. Before such instruments were used, they were blessed by a priest as a sign that the Church approved of whatever torture was about to be carried out.

This engraving from 1594 shows witches being tortured and executed in Trier.

The Witches' Sabbat

The Church taught that, at certain times of the year, groups of witches gathered together on mountaintops, in woods, or on bleak moors far from other people. Together, they performed frenzied dances until the Devil appeared, when they all feasted together. According to accounts given at witch trials, the food tasted terrible. These gatherings were named "sabbats," based on the word for the Sabbath, the Christian and Jewish holy day, because the witches were mocking Christian practices. Reports of these alleged gatherings fueled the fear of witches still further across Europe.

A ROYAL EXPERT

In 1604, shortly after King James VI of Scotland had also become king of England under the title James I, he introduced harsh new laws against witchcraft. The new king was a devoted Catholic, and was determined to stamp out witchcraft.

James had held the first mass witch trial in Scotland, at North Berwick, between 1590 and 1592. The king had tried to have his bride-to-be, Anne of Denmark, brought to Scotland from her native land, but storms had prevented her from sailing. The king decided the rough seas were the work of witches.

A woman named Geillis Duncan was arrested as a witch and tortured. She accused other local women of helping her cause the storms. Most of them were tortured until they also confessed to being witches.

King James I wrote a number of books, including a study of witchcraft.

The Devil's Marks

These illustrations include a witch casting a spell on people sleeping (*bottom*).

Duncan carried a "Devil's mark" on her neck, and many of the others who were arrested had similar marks. People believed that any facial blemish might show that a person was a witch. This included moles, warts, and fleabites, which very common at a time when few people washed regularly or did laundry. Any woman with sunken cheeks and hairy lips, or who was "crone-like" or "snaggle-toothed," or had crooked teeth, was thought to have the evil eye.

In all, about 70 people were put on trial in North Berwick. Many women were found guilty and hanged for witchcraft. A noble named the Earl of Bothwell, who was said to be behind a plan to prevent the king from marrying Anne of Denmark, was put on trial for treason. Because of his noble rank, he escaped with his life.

Writing About Witchcraft

In 1597, at the end of the trials in North Berwick, King James published a study of witchcraft named *Demonology*. The book included a list of the ways in which demons torture humans. It also described the activities of vampires and werewolves, and explained ideas about black magic. The book was part of the king's attempts to explain to his people why the Church should persecute witches.

17

CHAPTER 3
THE AGE OF THE WITCH HUNTERS

The witchcraft craze reached its peak in Europe in the seventeenth century. Tensions were high because of the religious wars that followed the Reformation which began in 1517. Christianity split into the Protestant and Catholic faiths, which fought for dominance. Both Churches accused their opponents of working with the Devil.

Following the Trier witch trials of the previous century, Germany was at the heart of the witch hunts. Three major witch trials took place in different cities: Fulda (1603–1606), Würzburg (1626–1631), and Bamberg (1626–1631). The trials resulted in the deaths of more than 1,000 people. The witch trials were part of the Thirty Years' War fought in Europe between 1618 and 1648. The conflict began as a fight between Protestants and Catholics but soon grew to a battle between the great European powers of the time. Witchcraft was a key battle zone.

In Bamberg, a harsh winter had left crops shrivelled and dead. Desperate to blame somebody, the region's Catholic rulers claimed witches had destroyed the harvest. They encouraged local peasants to turn on those suspected of witchcraft, killing women, men, and children. As the killings spread, however, people began to realize that they, too, might be arrested, tortured, and executed.

This painting shows a scene from the religious wars of the 1500s, a period of upheaval when violence against suspected witches was common.

Citizens turned against the rulers who had provoked the trials. When a woman from a leading family was executed despite an imperial order for her release, the trials were halted. They ended permanently when Protestant troops swept into Bamberg in 1632.

A Change of Heart

Even some Catholics began to have doubts about how much witchcraft actually existed. In Würzburg, the Jesuit priest Friedrich Spee was a confessor of witches, meaning that he heard them admit their sins under torture. Spee became convinced that the confessions were false, because they were obtained by torture. He secretly wrote a book stating his opinions, which he published anonymously in 1631 to avoid him being punished by the Church.

THE FRENCH POSSESSIONS

In seventeenth-century France, there were two cases of nuns accusing priests of sending demons to possess them. In both cases, the priests were found guilty and executed. Signs of the nuns' possession were recorded, and public exorcisms were held to drive out demons from the women.

Nuns were believed to be in particular danger of becoming possessed by demons.

In Aix-en-Provence in southern France in 1611, two nuns claimed that they had been bewitched by Father Louis Gaufridi. In turn, he accused them of being possessed by the Devil. When Sister Madeleine was about 16, she started to have shaking fits and visions of demonic creatures. An exorcism failed to get rid of her symptoms. She said Gaufridi had given her a green devil as a familiar.

Another young nun, Sister Louise, may have been jealous of the attention Madeleine gained for her claims of possession. Louise claimed that she was also possessed by 6,661 devils (666 was the "mark of the beast," or the Devil, according to the Bible).

Possessed by the Devil?

Sister Madeleine told tales of witches' sabbats where children were eaten, and she started to foam at the mouth. There was no proof that Gaufridi had done anything wrong, but he was arrested and tortured until he confessed to possessing the nuns. The priest was then executed.

A similar case involving nuns and a priest followed in Loudon in 1634. Again, the priest was found guilty and burned alive at the stake—even though he insisted he was innocent.

Father Urbain Grandier was strangled and burned at the stake for his involvement in witchcraft.

The Pendle Witches

In 1612, 12 people living on Pendle Hill in northern England were accused of killing 10 of their neighbors by witchcraft. The accused witches were tried along with a number of others in what became known as the Lancashire Witch Trial. Of the 12 from Pendle—nine women and two men—all but one were found guilty and executed by hanging.

21

WITCHFINDER GENERAL

During the Civil War in England (1642–1651), an unsuccessful lawyer named Matthew Hopkins became the most famous witch-hunter in England. Calling himself the Witchfinder General, even though it was not an official title, Hopkins traveled around eastern England looking for "witches." Paid for every arrest he made, Hopkins became wealthy until he was revealed as a fraud and forced to retire.

During a 14-month period in 1645 and 1646, Hopkins' activities led to 300 people being hanged for witchcraft. That was more women than had been hanged in England for witchcraft in the previous 100 years. It works out to more than 60 percent of the total number of people executed as witches throughout English history.

Matthew Hopkins's methods of identifying witches aroused a lot of opposition, including from clergy in the Anglican Church.

A Trick Stick

Hopkins used a "pricking test" to identify witches. The witch's body was stabbed with a sharp object to see if she felt pain. If the woman did not flinch or cry out, she was judged to be a witch. However, Hopkins used a trick pricking stick. When the tip pressed against someone's flesh, the blade pushed back into the handle, so the person was not actually pricked. That way, they did not feel pain or cry out—and were condemned as a witch.

Hopkins would jab his pricking stick against a Devil's mark on a woman and claim she was a witch. In one day, he condemned 68 people to death in this way. In one town, Hopkins was paid 900 times more for a single day's work than the average daily wage of the time.

This illustration shows Hopkins questioning suspected witches surrounded by their familiars.

The Swimming Test

One test used to identify witches was the "swimming test." This involved lowering an accused witch into a barrel of water or a pond. If she floated, then it was proof that she was a witch. If this happened, it was likely she would be executed. However, most people naturally float in water, so most people who were tested could not avoid being killed.

23

CHAPTER 4

DEMONS IN THE NEW WORLD

The Pilgrims landed in America at Cape Cod in Massachusetts Bay on November 11, 1620. They were in search of a new world where they could practice their own brand of Christianity, known as Puritanism. Puritans were Protestants who wanted to escape what they saw as the Catholic influence on the Church of England, even though it was a Protestant faith.

The Pilgrims gave thanks to God after landing in the "New World." They intended to keep that world free of any challenges to their Puritan faith.

The Puritans believed God would only allow a select few souls to achieve salvation, or be admitted into heaven. God had already decided who was going to be saved, but the Puritans said people must still lead a pure and good life to stand any chance of being admitted into heaven. That meant following strict rules that covered all aspects of life, including how often you went to church, how you dressed, and how you behaved.

Individuality was not allowed; everyone had to follow the same rules. Puritan preachers told their followers that God would severely punish anyone who did not follow those rules.

Witches Everywhere

In the new society the Puritans set up in Massachusetts, anyone who was considered "disobedient" or who did not show enough respect for Puritan rules was feared to be working with the Devil. Puritans believed that the Devil was as present in the world as God, and that the two were locked in a battle of good versus evil. According to their reasoning, anyone who committed a sin must be a follower of the Devil and was therefore probably a witch because, they argued, Devil worshippers included witches. The Puritans saw women as being inferior to men, and so more likely to be witches.

Under Puritan law, witchcraft was punishable by death. The punishment was strictly enforced in the Puritan colonies of New England in the seventeenth century, when hundreds of people were accused of witchcraft. The Salem trials of 1692 and 1693 were the most famous of the trials, but before they took place, 12 women had already been executed as witches in Massachusetts and Connecticut.

This illustration from seventeenth-century Massachusetts shows a witch collecting a plant to use in a potion.

A REVEALING CASE

In 1671, a young girl in the Massachusetts Bay Colony named Elizabeth Knapp was accused of being a witch. Knapp worked as a servant for the Reverend Samuel Willard. When she started to show signs of demonic possession, Willard observed her behavior and created a detailed record.

First Signs

Knapp first started to show signs of possession on October 30, 1671, and Willard recorded every episode until January 12, 1672. She grabbed at parts of her body, screamed, and went into jerking motions called convulsions. As she threw a fit, she called out "Money, money, sin and misery, misery." A physician could find no cause for her outbursts, but in one of her clearer moments, Knapp told Willard that she had made a pact with the Devil and let him take possession of her.

Witches Apprehended
...amined and Executed, for not...
villanies by them committed both by
Land and Water.
With a strange and most true triall how to...
whether a woman be a Witch
or not.

Printed at London for Edward Marchant,
be sold at his shop ouer against the Crosse
Church-yard. 1613.

The front of this pamphlet about witch trials has an illustration of a woman being ducked in water to test whether or not she is a witch.

A Detailed Diary

Willard was convinced that Knapp could not be faking her possession, because she seemed to be ready to harm herself. On one occasion, she even tried to throw herself into a fire. He concluded that her convulsions could only be the work of the Devil. After one last entry, however, he did not mention Elizabeth Knapp again. There are no records of what may have happened to her. Why she claimed to be possessed remains a mystery to this day. But Willard's notes of her behavior would have remarkable similarities with the later accounts of demonic possession from the Salem Witch Trials.

Grace Sherwood was executed as a witch—but pardoned by the governor of Virginia 300 years later.

IN MEMORY OF
GRACE WHITE SHERWOOD
1660 — 1740
HEALER OF SICK WITH HERBS
CONVICTED AS A WITCH
SHE SURVIVED VIRGINIA'S ONLY
TRIAL BY DUCKING IN THE
LYNNHAVEN RIVER
JULY 10, 1706
NAME CLEARED BY GOVERNOR
300 YEARS LATER

Trial by Ducking

In 1706, Grace Sherwood of Virginia was accused of being a witch. A jury of women examined her body for a hidden nipple said to be used to feed a familiar. When they did not find it, they decided to put her on a ducking stool to carry out the swimming test. A ducking stool, sometimes also called a cucking stool, was a long lever used to lower a woman into a pond or river. Sherwood floated, which was taken as proof she must be a witch, and was sentenced to seven years in jail. She was the only woman ever to be convicted in Virginia by "ducking."

THE SALEM WITCH TRIALS

The most famous of all colonial American witch trials were held in Salem in 1692 and 1693. An outbreak of demonic possession and accusations of witchcraft saw 20 people condemned to death while another five died in prison. Public reaction to the trials is said to have been responsible for turning America away from becoming a theocracy, or a country with a religious government.

The Possessions Begin

In the spring of 1692, a number of young girls in Salem, Massachusetts, claimed to be possessed by the Devil. Nine year-old Betty Parris and her 11-year-old cousin Abigail Williams started to have fits that seemed to support these claims. The girls made strange noises, adopted odd positions, including lying rigid in bed for hours, and threw things around the room. They also accused three local women of being witches. After the local physician could not find any explanation for their behavior, he declared that an evil force was at work. Salem was gripped by hysteria, which soon spread across the local area.

A Special Court

As more and more girls claimed to be possessed, a special court was held to try those accused of witchcraft. The first person to be tried, Bridget Bishop, was found guilty and hanged in June 1692. Following her execution, another 18 accused witches were tried, found guilty, and executed.

Over the next few months, another 150 women, men, and even children were accused of being possessed by the Devil. However, growing doubts about the way the trials were being conducted and about the weak evidence used to convict people led the governor of the colony to intervene. He wrote a pamphlet, published in London and Boston, that tried to dampen down the extreme hysteria about witchcraft. This helped to reduce tensions in Salem and the surrounding area. As the hysteria died down, the last witch trial was held in May 1693.

Betty Parris is shown here having a fit on the floor while Abigail Williams addresses the judges at a witch trial in Salem.

The trials at Salem remain one of the most notorious events in Massachusetts history. In November 2001, the Massachusetts legislature passed a bill pardoning some of those who had been executed for being witches.

CHAPTER 5

A WORLD OF DEMONS

The idea of demonic possession is common around the world. Unlike in Christian thinking, however, some cultures see being possessed as a sign that a person has special spiritual qualities. These individuals are sometimes of great importance in their communities.

Shamans

In tribal societies for the past 30,000 years, and still today, shamans have been important individuals or leaders. They are the connection between the spirit world and the tribe.

Also known as witch doctors or medicine men or women, their job is to use their abilities to heal the sick and to connect the living with the dead. They also influence natural phenomena, such as the weather.

In Africa, shaman often wear masks and costumes as they dance to try to contact the tribal spirits.

Native American Shamans

Native American tribes had their own shamans, such as Old Bear of the Mandan people of the Great Plains. To get into a trance-like state, these shamans usually starved themselves or spent time in very hot rooms full of steam. Shamans in India and South America use foods like special mushrooms or even alcohol to help them enter a trance.

The Spirit World

Shamans can be male or female, but more often than not they are men. To communicate with the spirit world, shamans go into a trance-like state that resembles demonic possession. They move in a different way and sound as though someone else is speaking through them. Some shamans claim to have a guardian spirit who gives them their power. While they are in a trance, shamans can communicate with spirits and gods, and use their power to perform acts to help the community, such as healing the sick or making the rains come so the crops grow.

This medicine man of the Iowya people was painted during a visit to London, England, in the 1840s.

During the shaman's trances, other members of the tribe carry out rituals to encourage the arrival of the spirits. Unlike with demonic possessions, these possessions are welcomed. During the rituals, there is music and dancing as well as eating and drinking.

31

VOODOO SPIRITS

On the Caribbean island of Haiti, many people follow a religion known as voodoo. Voodoo has its roots in Africa, and was brought to the Caribbean by Africans forced into slavery. Today, Haitian voodoo combines elements of Roman Catholicism with African religions to create its own special belief system.

Ancestral Spirits

In Haitian voodoo, priests and priestesses can be possessed by ancestral spirits known as loa, who are said to use them as their "horse." During voodoo rituals every Saturday, the priest or priestess calls on the loa to appear. The loa take all kinds of different forms. They can be full of energy and cause their "horse" to thrash about or even to go into fits.

This Haitian painting depicts Dambala, the most powerful of the loa, who created the world.

The way the priest or priestess acts during a possession reflects the character of the loa. Someone possessed by a snake-like spirit such as Dambala will writhe on the floor, for example. Once the loa is recognized, worshippers make appropriate offerings to it to help the ritual go well.

Christian Echoes

Haiti has a deeply religious and superstitious culture. Possession by an loa is seen as being similar to the demonic possession described in the Bible. This reflects the forced conversion of slaves to Christianity when they arrived on the island from the sixteenth century onward.

Possessed Warriors

In late-medieval Europe, Viking warriors would go into a state of possession before they went into battle or on a raid. They named it *berserkergang*, which means "going beserk." The warriors worked themselves up until they started to shiver, their teeth chattered, and their faces went bright red. In battle, the warriors howled like animals, bit their shields, and lashed out like wild beasts. After fighting, they went into a deep sleep for a day or longer. This is the origin of the word berserk.

ISLAM AND JINNS

In the early Arab world and in the Islamic religion, which began in the 600s, people could become possessed by evil spirits called *jinns*, also known as genies. Jinns belonged to the supernatural world; if they were not treated correctly, they could harm people. The word "jinn" comes from the Arabic verb "*janna*," meaning to hide or to conceal. Like demons and spirits, jinns are invisible to the human eye.

Origins of Jinns

Just as demons are mentioned in the Christian Bible, the holy book of Islam, the Koran, mentions jinns: "Indeed We created man from dried clay of black smooth mud. And We created the Jinn before that from the smokeless flame of fire" (Koran: 15:26–27). The fact that jinns were created from a flame suggests that they were fiery by nature, with supernatural powers that far exceed those of humans. According to the Koran, jinns were created before humankind but after the angels.

In this illustration of a traditional tale from the Middle East, a jinn in the shape of a jackal (*right*) tries to trick the lion-king.

Becoming Visible

Some people believe jinns originate in a parallel universe to our own. Like humans, jinns can marry, have children, and live much as humans do, apart from the fact that they can live a very long time. Like demons, jinns can possess people, animals, or even vegetation, such as trees, by taking on their form.

According to Islamic teaching, the aim of jinns is to try to trick people into worshipping beings other than the Muslim god. This is considered sacrilegious, or a crime against religious law. In order to expel the spirit of a jinn, a devout Muslim must say special verses from the Koran that call on God for assistance to drive the demon out.

In the story of Aladdin, when Aladdin rubs a magic lamp, a jinn appears and grants Aladdin his wishes.

1001 Arabian Nights

A collection of Middle Eastern folk stories, *Arabian Nights*, also called *The Thousand and One Nights*, was written down during the Golden Age of Islam from the eighth to fourteenth centuries. The collection has several tales featuring jinns. They include the story of Aladdin, whose magic lamp contained a jinn that was released when he rubbed it.

CHAPTER 6

POSSESSIONS TODAY

During the twentieth century, the idea of demons and possession became a common feature of horror books and movies such as *The Exorcist*. In some smaller churches—particularly some small African churches—the idea of possession is still highly feared. Priests still carry out exorcisms, although today many people condemn this practice as unnecessary and cruel.

The Horror Genre

During the 1960s and 1970s, a number of novels were published that described demonic possession. They were so popular that some were made into movies, which brought the stories to an even wider audience. These books included *The Exorcist* (1971) by William Peter Blatty, Ira Levin's *Rosemary's Baby* (1967), and *The Shining* (1977) by Stephen King.

In *The Exorcist* movie, a priest dies when the demon throws him down these steps.

The Exorcist

The Exorcist tells the story of a 12-year-old girl possessed by an ancient demon and the two priests who try to exorcise it. Blatty wrote the book after he heard about a similar case while he was a student at Georgetown University. Two years after the novel was published, it was made into one of the most profitable of all horror movies. The movie had a huge influence on popular culture. The movies of both *Rosemary's Baby* and *The Shining* are also widely watched every Halloween.

The author Stephen King was inspired to write the novel *The Shining* after his stay at the Stanley Hotel in Colorado.

Ndoki

In some African churches, as well as a few outside Africa, people believe children can be possessed by demons. They believe children become possessed in the womb or by eating some infected food. In the Lingala language of Central Africa, these children are known as "ndoki," or "witches." To free ndoki of their evil spirits, a pastor and church elders whisper prayers in children's ears to force the spirit to leave. In a few cases, however, the exorcism rituals are reported to have ended in the death of the child.

37

A FAMOUS HOAX

In 1735, during the reign of George II, Great Britain introduced a new law called the Witchcraft Act. The act was not aimed at prosecuting witches, because by then most people believed that witchcraft did not exist. The new act targeted people who claimed to be witches. It meant they could now be prosecuted for fraud, or pretending something was true.

The Witchcraft Act remained law in Great Britain until 1951. In 1944, it led to a sensational trial that reached England's highest criminal court, the Old Bailey. A Scottish medium named Helen Duncan became one of the last people to be prosecuted under the Witchcraft Act.

Duncan held séances during World War II (1939–1945) in the naval town of Portsmouth in southern England. Families who were desperate to know news of missing loved ones, many whom had been lost at sea, attended Duncan's séances hoping to talk to their missing relatives. They happily paid the fee Duncan charged for her séances.

People who claim to tell the future using methods such as looking into a crystal ball are often accused of being frauds.

Duncan's fraud was based on people's desire to find out what happened to their loved ones during the war.

Exposing the Fraud

During one séance, two naval officers switched seats as a test. Duncan had learned information about the people attending the séance, but she did not realize the men had moved. She told each man the information she had learned about the other's family. The men reported her as a fraud, so the police sent undercover officers to another séance. A sailor at the séance claimed to recognize the voice of a spirit who "spoke" through Duncan as that of his dead mother. The spirit appeared, carrying what appeared to be a dead baby, who was supposed to be the sailor. The police officers grabbed the "spirit," who turned out to be an accomplice of Duncan's. The "baby" was in fact a bundle of white cloth.

A Con Woman

After her arrest, Helen Duncan was put on trial and was found guilty in just 24 minutes. It turned out that she had previous convictions for fraud and that her latest scam, the séances, were making her a huge amount of money every week. She was sentenced to nine months in jail. The Witchcraft Act was only used once more, later that same year. After that, people like Mrs. Duncan were charged with fraud.

39

A SERIAL KILLER

During a 12-month reign of terror between 1976 and 1977, a serial killer who named himself "Son of Sam" murdered six people and wounded seven in New York City. When David Berkowitz was arrested, he confessed to the murders but claimed that he was working on the orders of a demon that inhabited a dog named Harvey. The dog belonged to Berkowitz's neighbor, Sam Carr.

David Berkowitz shot his victims with a revolver. He left letters promising more attacks—and terrified New Yorkers.

Berkowitz pleaded guilty and was sentenced to 365 years in jail, but the trial left many unanswered questions. When Berkowitz was asked his name in court, he replied, "My name is Legion, for we are many." This refers to an episode in the New Testament when Christ asks a man who is possessed for his name, and the man replies, "My name is Legion, for we are many." Was Berkowitz suggesting that he was also possessed by demons?

The Mystery Deepens

Messages Berkowitz wrote on the walls of his home and letters he sent to the police and press suggested he was involved in a satanic cult. It seemed that he got a job in a dog pound so he could steal dogs for a cult in upstate New York. The cult killed the dogs as part of their witchcraft rituals. It seemed that Berkowitz might have not acted alone.

Berkowitz's neighbor, Sam Carr, was a hippy with fair hair while Berkowitz had dark hair. Several witnesses to the crimes said the killer had been fair-haired. The police also suspected that more than one person had been involved in the murders because of differences in the way the victims were shot. They tried to locate Carr, but by the time they found him in North Dakota, he was dead, having apparently shot himself. Painted on his hand was the number 666, the mark of Satan, and scrawled on the wall was "SSNYC"—Son of Sam, New York City.

Berkowitz was said to be associated with cults that carried out black-magic rituals.

41

DEVIL IN THE COURTS

In 1981, Arne Cheyenne Johnson became the first person to defend himself in a US court by saying that he had been forced to commit a crime by demonic possession. He claimed a demon had made him murder his landlord.

Possession on Trial

On February 16, 1981, 18-year-old Arne Cheyenne Johnson fatally stabbed his landlord, Alan Bono. At his trial, Johnson claimed that the death was the fault of a demon that had recently possessed him.

Johnson claimed that the demon was living in an old well—but the jury did not believe him.

Johnson told the court that his girlfriend's 11-year-old brother, David Glatzel, had been taken over by a demon on a property Johnson was planning to rent out. David started to have night terrors and became covered in unexplained bruises and scratches. A Catholic priest who examined the house said that an evil spirit was present. The spirit presented itself as an old man. Johnson claimed to have tried to divert the demon that was tormenting David.

Rejected Defense

Johnson said that the demon possessed him instead of David. Johnson's girlfriend said that his behavior changed from then on. He began to fall into trances and make odd noises, but had no recollection of the incidents afterward.

The jury did not believe Johnson's story of demonic possession. He was found guilty of manslaughter rather than murder, but only because he also claimed that he acted in self-defense when he killed Bono. Johnson was sentenced to between 10 and 20 years in jail.

After thousands of years of fear of possession, it seemed that modern society had come to reject such beliefs—although for a few people, the dangers remain as real as ever.

Australian Demon

In 2018, Australian Alex McEwan also used demonic possession as a defense in his trial for murder. In 2013, he had killed a Korean exchange student, Eunji Ban, in a random attack in Brisbane, Australia. McEwan claimed he was forced to attack Ban by a demon that had accompanied him since the age of 6. The demon, which he called Jazzy, had horse-like legs, a goat's head, and horns. The jury rejected McEwan's defense and sentenced him to life in prison.

43

TIMELINE

380 — The Roman Empire makes Christianity its official religion.

415 — The scholar Hypatia is murdered after rival scholars accuse her of witchcraft.

c.1450 — The mass persecution of witches begins in Europe.

1484 — Pope Innocent VIII denounces witchcraft as a sin against the Church.

1487 — *The Hammer of Witches* is published. The book is a guide to identifying and punishing witches, and is very biased against women.

1563 — A new law makes witchcraft punishable by death in England.

1566 — Agnes Waterhouse becomes the first person to be executed as a witch in England under the new law.

1581 — Mass witch trials start in the region of Trier in Germany.

1590 — Witch trials begin at North Berwick, Scotland, after King James VI accuses his enemies of using witchcraft to prevent his marriage.

1597 — King James VI publishes *Demonology*. It hardens attitudes against witches.

1611 — Aix-en-Provence holds the first of a series of witch trials in France.

1618 — The Thirty Years' War begins in Europe. This religious conflict between Catholics and Protestants sees witch persecutions at a peak.

1645 — Matthew Hopkins becomes Witchfinder General in England. In just two years he uses fraud to have 300 victims executed for witchcraft.

1692 — Witch trials begin in Salem, Massachusetts, that lead to the executions of 19 people.

1736 — New laws in Great Britain remove the harshest penalties for witchcraft.

1944 — Helen Duncan becomes the second last person in Britain to be convicted of witchcraft.

1951 — The Witchcraft Act is repealed in Britain.

1971 — *The Exorcist* sparks a new genre of books and movies based on demons.

1981 — Arne Cheyenne Johnson uses demonic possession as a defense during his trial for murder.

2018 — Alex McEwan claims to have been possessed when he murdered Eunji Ban in Brisbane in 2013. He is sentenced to life imprisonment.

GLOSSARY

amulets Charms that protect their wearers from harm.

anonymously Without using a name.

astronomer Someone who studies space.

blemish A small mark or flaw.

cult A small religious group with views that are seen as extreme or odd.

curse A call for a supernatural power to harm someone.

eternity The whole of time.

executed Killed as a punishment.

exorcisms Religious rituals intended to drive demons out of people.

fits Uncontrollable jerking of the body.

flinch To make an automatic movement away from a possible threat.

fraud An illegal deception carried out to make money.

frenzy Uncontrolled excitement.

hoax A deliberate deception.

hysteria Uncontrollable emotion or excitement.

imperial Related to an empire.

individuality The state of people being very different from everyone else.

infected Carrying germs that can cause disease or other harm.

magic The power to control events using supernatural forces.

medium Someone who claims to be able to communicate with the dead.

mob A large crowd of people.

mocking Making fun of something.

moles Small, dark spots on the skin.

pamphlet A small booklet or leaflet.

pardoned Excused for a crime.

peasants Very poor people who used to work on the land.

persecute To treat a group of people badly because of their religious beliefs.

phenomena Observable events.

philosopher Someone who thinks deeply about complex subjects.

potions Liquids with healing or magical qualities.

prosecuted Charged with a crime.

Puritanism A very strict form of the Protestant faith.

rituals Religious ceremonies that follow a strict order of actions.

satanic Related to the worship of the Devil, or Satan.

séances Meetings held to try to contact the dead.

supernatural Not explained by science or the laws of nature.

superstition A belief that is not based on reason.

torment Severe suffering.

tortured Made to suffer pain, usually to get someone to confess something.

trance A dream-like state.

treason The crime of trying to overthrow a government.

underworld A place where the dead are believed to carry on existing.

vampires Dead bodies said to leave their graves at night to drink blood.

werewolves People who sometimes change into wolves.

witches People thought to have evil magical powers.

woodcut A print made by carving a design into a piece of wood.

FOR FURTHER READING

BOOKS

Burgan, Michael. *The Salem Witch Trials: Mass Hysteria and Many Lives Lost* (Tangled History). North Mankato, MN: Capstone Press, 2019.

Shoup, Kate. *Ghosts, Posessions, and Unexplained Presences* (Paranormal Investigations). New York, NY: Cavendish Square, 2017.

Weiner, Danielle. *Investigating Angels and Demons* (Understanding the Paranormal). New York, NY: Rosen Education Service, 2016.

Wood, Alix. *Witch Trials* (Why'd They Do That? Strange Customs of the Past). New York, NY: Gareth Stevens Publishing, 2018.

WEBSITES

Jinns—*www.britannica.com/topic/jinni*
Details about the demons described in the Islamic faith.

Witchcraft—*people.howstuffworks.com/witchcraft.htm*
The history of witchcraft and the persecution of witches.

Witches—*https://www.worldbooklearning.com/10-facts-about -the-history-of-witchcraft*
Facts about witches and witchcraft.

Witchfinder General—*www.historic-uk.com/HistoryUK/ HistoryofEngland/Matthew-Hopkins-WitchFinder-General*
The story of Matthew Hopkins in England.

INDEX